First World War
and Army of Occupation
War Diary
France, Belgium and Germany

25 DIVISION
Divisional Troops
Divisional Cyclist Company
25 September 1915 - 18 April 1916

WO95/2233/2

The Naval & Military Press Ltd
www.nmarchive.com
Published in association with The National Archives

Published by

The Naval & Military Press Ltd

Unit 10 Ridgewood Industrial Park,

Uckfield, East Sussex,

TN22 5QE England

Tel: +44 (0) 1825 749494

www.naval-military-press.com

www.nmarchive.com

This diary has been reprinted in facsimile from the original. Any imperfections are inevitably reproduced and the quality may fall short of modern type and cartographic standards.

© Crown Copyright
Images reproduced by permission of The National Archives, London, England, 2015.

Contents

Document type	Place/Title	Date From	Date To
Heading	WO95/2233/2 Divisional Cyclist Company		
Heading	25th Divl Cyclist Coy. Sep 1915-Apr 1916		
Heading	25th. Divl: Cycl: Coy: Vol I Sept & Oct. 15-Apr 16		
War Diary	Farnborough	25/09/1915	25/09/1915
War Diary	Southampton	25/09/1915	25/09/1915
War Diary	Havre	26/09/1915	26/09/1915
War Diary	Steenbecque	27/09/1915	27/09/1915
War Diary	Strazeele	28/09/1915	30/09/1915
War Diary	Bailleul	01/10/1915	02/10/1915
War Diary	Rabot-W Nieppe	03/10/1915	08/10/1915
War Diary	Ploegsteert Le Touquet	08/10/1915	11/10/1915
War Diary	Rabot	12/10/1915	26/10/1915
War Diary	Bailleul	27/10/1915	27/10/1915
War Diary	Nieppe	28/10/1915	28/10/1915
War Diary	Rabot	29/10/1915	31/10/1915
Heading	25th. Divl. Cyclist Vol. 2 Nov 15.		
War Diary	Rabot	01/11/1915	01/11/1915
War Diary	Ploegsteert	01/11/1915	07/11/1915
War Diary	Rabot	07/11/1915	30/11/1915
Heading	25th. Divl: Cyclist Vol: 3. Dec 15		
War Diary	Rabot	01/12/1915	04/12/1915
War Diary	Ploegsteert	04/12/1915	09/12/1915
War Diary	Rabot	09/12/1915	24/12/1915
War Diary	Ploegsteert	24/12/1915	29/12/1915
War Diary	Rabot	29/12/1915	31/12/1915
Heading	25th. Div. Cyclist Coy. January 1916.		
Heading	25th. Divl: Cyclist Vol: 4 Jan 16		
War Diary	Rabot	01/01/1916	03/01/1916
War Diary	Ploegsteert	03/01/1916	07/01/1916
War Diary	Rabot	07/01/1916	07/01/1916
War Diary	Clair Marais	08/01/1916	18/01/1916
War Diary	Rabot	08/01/1916	13/01/1916
War Diary	Ploegsteert	13/01/1916	19/01/1916
War Diary	Rabot	19/01/1916	24/01/1916
War Diary	Merris	24/01/1916	31/01/1916
Heading	25th. Div. Cyclist Coy. February 1916.		
War Diary	Merris	01/02/1916	29/02/1916
Heading	25th. Div. Cyclist Coy. March 1916.		
War Diary	Merris	01/03/1916	09/03/1916
War Diary	Busmes	10/03/1916	10/03/1916
War Diary	Sachin	11/03/1916	16/03/1916
War Diary	Bryas	17/03/1916	31/03/1916
Heading	25th. Div. Cyclist Coy. April 1916.		
War Diary	Bryas	01/04/1916	04/04/1916
War Diary	Averdoingt	05/04/1916	18/04/1916

WO/95/2233/2

Dunsurened Cyclist Company

25TH DIVISION
DIVL TROOPS

25TH DIVL CYCLIST COY.
SEP 1915-APR 1916

121/7608

25th Divl: Cycl: Cor:
vol I

Sept. & Oct. 15
ap. 16

Army Form C. 2118.

WAR DIARY
or
INTELLIGENCE SUMMARY. [Raiul]

(Erase heading not required.)

SEPTEMBER 1915

Hour, Date, Place		Summary of Events and Information	Remarks and references to Appendices
1.20 pm	25 September. FARNBOROUGH	Entrained for foreign service.	
7.0 - 7.0 pm	SOUTHAMPTON	Embarked on "S.S. KING EDWARD"; cycles in company transport on "S.S. MAIDAN".	
1.30 am	26.		
7.0 am	HAVRE	arrived in dock.	
		disembarked and marched to Quay "O", where the Company stayed all day, doing fatigue work on "S.S. MAIDAN".	
6.0 pm		Marched to Pt. I. for entraining. Having entrained & proceeded via ABBEVILLE — BOULOGNE — CALAIS — ST OMER — HAZEBROUCK — STEEN BECQUE.	
6.30 pm	STAINBECQUE.	Detained, and marched via roads & rode W. by STRAZEELE to Pt. SEE BOIS	had to leave cooker-cart owing to broken axle. Eventually follow in this
11.30 pm	STEENZEELE	in PRADELLES.	form.
2.0 pm	28.	moved ¼ mile South.	
	28 - 30.	In billets	

Reginald [illegible] Capt.
COMMANDING.
XXVᵗʰ DIVISIONAL CYCLIST COMPANY.

HEAD QUARTERS
XXXV DIVISIONAL CYCLIST COMPANY
8 NOV 1915
No. 1

Army Form C. 2118.

WAR DIARY
or
INTELLIGENCE SUMMARY.
(Erase heading not required.)

OCTOBER 1915

Hour, Date, Place	Summary of Events and Information	Remarks and references to Appendices
1.30 p.m. 1st October. BAILLEUL.	Moved to Billets about ½ mile S.W. of BAILLEUL, on the BAILLEUL – VIEUX BERQUIN road.	1st: 2 men attached to Signal Co. XXV Division.
2.0 p.m. 2nd	Conference for Company Commanders at BAILLEUL.	1 N.C.O. at manœuvres 198. Co. A.P.C.
1.30 p.m. 3rd RABOT – to – NIEPPE	Moved to Billets, ½ mile N.E. of STEENWERCKE, nr/a STEENWERCKE – RABOT road.	3rd: Driver to A.P.M. and daily since.
4" – 7"	In Billets. Patrols at daily learning the area, and fatigue duties.	6th: 1 N.C.O. to J.P. attached of 1 N.C.O. 27 mach. attle. to C.R.E. daily. All Batteries above cancelled. 6/10/15.
3. 15 p.m. 8"	Capt. G.L. Andrew, Lieut. W.C. Collins and 2/Lieut. DR. Bailey and C.L. Blake, Serjeants and Corporals of the Battn. No. 113 and 6 Platoons left to 2/. have instruction in trench duties. No. 1 to 6 attached to 8th Battn. Border Regt. 75th Infantry Brigade. Coys Nos 8 to 13th Battn. CHESHIRE Regt. 7th Infantry Brigade. The latter had a hostile bombardment for about one hour.	8th: 2 men to salvage Co. XXV.D.
6.0 p.m. 9"	Capt. Reg. Middleton, 2/Lieut. S.M.C. Naughton, with Serjeants and Corporals of Nos 2 & 5 Platoons relieved those with 7th Infantry Bde. attached to "C" and "D" Coys 10th Battn. CHESHIRE Regt. 2/Lieut. R. Stephenson with Serjeants and Corporals No 4 Platoon relieved those in 74th Infantry Bde.	
6.0 p.m. 10"	Nos. 1 and 6 Platoons under Lieut. Collins relieved to members of "C" & "D" Coys 10th Battn. Cheshire Regiment, and held trenches 102-3, 106-7. Lieut. Coy and No. 3 Platoon under Capt. Andrew attached to No. 1 Coy 13th Battn. Cheshire Regiment.	
6.0 p.m. 11"	Nos 2 & 5 Platoons under Lieut. Littt. Lindsay relieved No. 1 & 6. and 2 sections No. 6, who stayed into refuge No. 2. No. 4 Platoon under 2/Lieut. Stephenson relieved No. 3.	
12" RABOT.	in Billets. Patrolling area.	13th: 15 Rank, file to A.R.M. for control posts. 1 Sgt & 27 men to C.R.E.

over Sheet 2.

Forms/C. 2118/10

Army Form C. 2118.

WAR DIARY
or
INTELLIGENCE SUMMARY.
(Erase heading not required.)

Instructions regarding War Diaries and Intelligence Summaries are contained in F. S. Regs., Part II. and the Staff Manual respectively. Title pages will be prepared in manuscript.

OCTOBER 1915

Hour, Date, Place			Summary of Events and Information	Remarks and references to Appendices
2.30 P.M	13th October	RABOT	in Billets. Lieut. J.M.C. Houghton, and 23 other ranks sent to A.P.M. to act as Battle Patrols at end of trenches ; during demonstration on our front.	13th. 1 man J.P. struck off
	14th – 20th		in Billets. a fatigue.	16th. 1 man returned from Sig. Cy.
	20th		in Billets. 2nd Lieut. C.H. Blake and 4 men detached to form Observation posts along our front and billeted in PLOEGSTEERT.	17th. increased control posts to 27. O.R.
	22nd — 24th		reconnoitred area from RENCHES to ROMARIN in view of an emergency way to RENCHES in view of an attack, roads being impassable. Capt. Régis Neuton. Cpl Andrews. Lieuts W.E. Collins & JWE Lindsay ; and 2 Lieuts D.S. Bayley and J.M.C. Houghton, and certain NCOs carried the work out.	18th. 1 man J.P. struck off. 21st. 1 N.C.O & 20 O.R. to A.O.D. (re case fatigue 3 canulus) 22nd. 1 N.C.O & 30 O.R. to A.O.D. 23rd. 1 N.C.O & 40 O.R. to Baths Nieppe. A.O.D fatigue daily in future
	25th 26th		in Billets. a fatigue.	25th.
11.0 a.m.	27th	BAILLEUL	Capt. Reg. W. Neuton and 20 other ranks paraded as representative detachment of the Company. This party formed rendezvous near NIEPPE of Divisional representative Battalion and one platoon of "A" Company of the Brigade troops Corps (III Army Corps) met the representative Divisional Cyclist Coy. BAILLEUL. at 2.30 p.m. The Brigade marched past H.M. George V. lining the main road to BAILLEUL and giving three cheers as he drove away.	
12.0 noon	28th	NIEPPE	Gas ammunition. (Parade state 5 officers represented all available in company) Remainder in fatigue.	28th. 2 N.C.O & 50 O.R. to CRE ditto.
	29th – 30th	RABOT	in Billets. fatigue.	29th.
	31st.		went to Bttn Q. ; 7th Bns DLI. and Nth.8. and Nth.8. 6th Battn. L.N. Lancs. Reg. to get in trenches re taking over trenches on 1.XI.15	30th. 1 N.C.O & 7th 5th.

Reginald Neulon Captn
COMMANDING XXTH DIVISIONAL CYCLIST COMPANY

HEAD QUARTERS
8 NOV 1915
XXTH DIVISIONAL CYCLIST COMPANY

25th Oct. Exhib.
vol. 2

121/7656

Nov 15.

Army Form C. 2118.

WAR DIARY
or
INTELLIGENCE SUMMARY.

(Erase heading not required.)

NOVEMBER 1915.

Hour, Date, Place		Summary of Events and Information	Remarks and references to Appendices
RABOT.	1st Nov. 8⁰⁰ am	Capt. Reg. M. Newton. Lieuts J.T.C. Lindsay and W.F. Collins with 100 other ranks marched to PROUQSTEURT WOOD	2 men R.P.M. 1 – 30 mm 10 " Radha 1 – 30 " 27 " Control 1 – 2 " (ormerly) (I. ach)
PROUQSTEURT.	1st – 7th	relieved "C" Coy 8/L.N.L. Lancs. in support line (FORT BOYD, MOATED FARM, HUNTERS AVENUE LIDEAD HORSE (CORNER). HdQrs DURHAM H.O.) Lieut Wills 7th Bn	8½ joint 2 A30 @ 50 mm – CRE 11 " 1 N30 . 10 " – A.O.D. 13 " 1 permanently to Sanitary Squad
	7th Nov. 9⁰⁰ am	relieved by "B" Coy 8/L.N.L. Lancs in B. trench	1 . 30 . to Div Rest Billet 11½ " 1 N30 mm A.O.D.
RABOT	7 – 13	Lieut. W.F. Collins Lieuts F.B. Bathy & R.Stevenson. with Y Coy relieve "B" Coy 8/L.N.L. Reg	
	13th Nov.	Capt. G.L. Andrew went to Technical School. with 45 Div J. Rivers Dinghe return takes over Divisional Technical School.	
	15th Nov.	½ Coy relieved by "D" Coy 8/L.N.L. Reg	
RABOT	19th Nov	In Billets.	
	19 – 24	Capt. Reg. M. Newton. Lieut J.T.C. Lindsay & Lieut. Houghton at ½ Coy relieved "D" Coy 8/L.N.L. Reg.	
	24th	relieved by "A" Coy 8/L.N.L. Reg	
RABOT.	25th	In billets	
	29 – 30	Grenadier Platoon formed under Lieut. F.M.C. Houghton.	

Regin Newton
COMMANDING.
XXVth DIVISIONAL CYCLIST COMPANY.

25" Stil: Cyclob"
vol: 3.

121/7796

Keck 15

Army Form C. 2118.

WAR DIARY
or
INTELLIGENCE SUMMARY

(Erase heading not required.)

Instructions regarding War Diaries and Intelligence Summaries are contained in F.S. Regs., Part II. and the Staff Manual respectively. Title pages will be prepared in manuscript.

DECEMBER 1915.

Hour, Date, Place	Summary of Events and Information	Remarks and references to Appendices
1st – 3rd. RABOT.	in Billets. "Grenadier training". 2/Lieut. HOUGHTON a fatigues	1st – 5th: Div. Tech. Schul. 1 NCO. & 72 men
		10 – 11th: " " " 1 NCO. 10 men
4th – 9th. PLOEGSTEERT.	Capt. Reg. W. NEWTON., Lieut. W.E. COLLINS, 2/Lieut. F.B. BAYLY Interaunay, Interchange with and 2/Lieut. F.A.G. HOUGHTON	12 – 13th: " " " 1 NCO. 10 men
	and 100 Other ranks relieved "A" Coy. 9/Royal North Lancs. in support line.	20 – 28th: " " " 2 NCOs 18 men
	(Fort Boyd etc.) Sending Sergt. Jones and 10 men to "A" Coy. Yearg STEENWERK	24 – 30: 1 NCO. 30 men
	and 10 "B" Coy, Sergt Edwards and 10 men to "C" Coy. Sergt Doyle and 10	10 – 20 Nieppe Sq. 1 NCO. 20 men
	men of "D" Coy. 6/Wilts Regt. in the front line. In 1st place men	13: 1 NCO. 20 men
	withdrawn to take places in a "cut out" expedition. (This took place in the	
	7th inst.) and were not involved.	13 – 27th: Div. Rear Billet.
9th – 21st. RABOT.	in Billets. "Grenadier training: fatigues.	1 OR to cattle quarantine
20th.	Divisional "Guides" formed under 2/Lieut. F.B. BAYLY. 16. O.R.	15th: 1. OR to Grave Registration Commn. BAILLEUL (permanent)
	"Grenadiers" temporarily reduced 24 O.R.	
21st. – 29th. PLOEGSTEERT.	Lieut. W.E. COLLINS and 35 O.R. and 2/Lieut. R. STEPHENSON and	16th: Coal Dump STEENWERCK.
	25 O.R. to "C" Coy. Sergt Jones and 10 O.R. 6 "D" Coy 6/Wilts in front	a corps Guards (permanent)
	line.	10th – 3.10th ww.
29th – 31st. RABOT.	in Billets:—	Corpl. M.
		2. OR. Signals
		1 OR Bombing School
		1 OR Rear Billet
" 21st"		1 OR. Sanitary Section
	1 NCO and 7 men sent as "Artillery Observers" and attached to	2 OR Salvage
	21st Division	Observation Dist. 10/Men & men
		Total. 27. OR.

Regn. Newton Major
COMMANDING.
XXVth DIVISIONAL CYCLIST COMPANY.

[Stamp: HEAD QUARTERS XXVth DIVISIONAL CYCLIST COMPANY 31 DEC 1915]

25th. DIVISIONAL CYCLISTS

25th. DIV. CYCLIST COY.

JANUARY 1916.

25th Divl: Cyclist
Vol: 4
Jan '16

Army Form C. 2118.

WAR DIARY
or
INTELLIGENCE SUMMARY.
(Erase heading not required.)

JANUARY 1916.

Instructions regarding War Diaries and Intelligence Summaries are contained in F.S. Regs., Part II. and the Staff Manual respectively. Title pages will be prepared in manuscript.

Hour, Date, Place	Summary of Events and Information	Remarks and references to Appendices
RABOT. 1–3rd January 1916.	In billets. Divisional Guides (min. No. 4) under Lieut. J.B. BAYLY.	Practice Control posts 1st/2nd 20 OR. 2 OR. 3rd/4th " 14 " 22nd/23rd 9 "
ROEGSTEERT. 3rd–7th January	Lieut. J.M.Z. LINDESAY and 25 OR. to "C" Coy. P.B. WILTS, and Sergt Edwards & 24 OR to "B" Coy. within front line trenches.	Div Technical School field 4th/5th Y. 1 NCO 9th/10th 10 " Y. NCO 20 — C RE fare Brushwood fatigue 9 NCO & 6 —
RABOT 7th Jan. CLAIR MARAIS 8th – 18th Jan.	In billets. Lieut. J.M.Z. LINDESAY and 15 OR. (a party of XXV Division) party to CLAIR MARAIS near ST OMER.	Observation duties 3rd/4th 20m 10 10 OR. " 21st/22nd 1.O. 11 OR. 22nd/23rd 1.O. 10 OR. 24th/25th 8 OR
RABOT 8th – 13th	Remainder of Company in Billets.	Battle Pt. Patrols 8th 1 NCO 10 men " 9th 1 NCO 25 men " 11th 1 NCO 20 men 13th 1 NCO 10 men
ROEGSTEERT. 13th – 19th Jany.	2/Lieut F.M.J. HOUGHTON and 20 OR to "B" Coy 1st Batt. Serg Bunting and 19 OR to "C" Coy in front line.	Orderlies. To A.P.M. 13th/14th 2 OR. 30th/31st 1 OR. Signal Coy 13th/14th 1 OR. " 30th/31st 1 OR. Salvage Coy 13th/14th 2 OR. Div Rest Billets 13th 1 OR. " Sanitary Officer 13th 1 OR. " Bathing School 13th 1 OR. " Graves Regn Coy 23rd 1 OR.
RABOT 19th – 24th Jany.	In billets.	Guard Gal Jump 1st/2nd 24 4 OR Div Technical Sch. 17th/23rd 1 O. 1 OR.
MERRIS. 24th Jan. 9:30 am.	Lorries hq: Divisional Cyclist Company. the Company moved back via LA CRÊCHE, NOOTE BOOME to Billets 400 yds N of "E" in MERRIS. In Billets 2nd Corps Reserve.	
24th – 31st Jany.		

Rgn Newton Capt
COMMANDING.
XXVTH DIVISIONAL CYCLIST COMPANY.

25th. DIVISIONAL CYCLISTS

25th. DIV. CYCLIST COY.

F E B R U A R Y   1 9 1 6.

WAR DIARY

INTELLIGENCE SUMMARY.

(Erase heading not required.)

Army Form C. 2118.

FEBRUARY 1916.

Hour, Date, Place	Summary of Events and Information	Remarks and references to Appendices
MERRIS 1st – 29th	In billets. 2nd Corps Reserve. Training of Company and Specialists &c.	Capt. Andrew (1st General) S/Staff (Capt. 75th Inf. Bde. 4 – 29 . 2 . 16.
9th 10.0 a.m.	Marched past G.O.C. II Army in Field Service Marching Order.	1 Cpl 27 men with 21st Div. Arty. on rotation from 1 – 29th
12th –	But on 4 hrs notice to move	2 men Boulogne. 1 – 29
13th –	4 hrs notice cancelled	1 – Div Rest Station. 1 – 4th
27th –	2/Lieut Blake & 4 men went to ARMENTIÈRES to take over observation posts from 21st Division on relief.	Sig Office. 1 – 29 Div Rest Stat. 1 – 29 Signals Co. 1 – 29
26th –	But on 9 hrs notice to move by rail, and relief of 21st Div cancelled.	Spare Regt. 1 – 29 18th Co. A.S.C. 2 – 29 A.P.M. Onealy 1 – 29
29th –	2/Lieut Blake & 4 men returned from ARMENTIÈRES.	6 men instructors repair Gum Boots by Div D.O.S. 9 – 14th 3 men Sanitary Det. 21 – 29th 2 Cpls sel instrl Reinft. Camp R.E. 27th 3 men from A.S.C. – attached to 2 W. Surrey Coy.

Renewed 3/3/16

Rawlinson Captn.
COMMANDING
XXVth DIVISION CYCLIST COMPANY.

R.W.

25th. DIVISIONAL CYCLISTS

25th. DIV. CYCLIST COY.

MARCH 1916.

COPY of
WAR DIARY
or
INTELLIGENCE SUMMARY
(Erase heading not required.)

Instructions regarding War Diaries and Intelligence Summaries are contained in F.S. Regs., Part II. and the Staff Manual respectively. Title Pages will be prepared in manuscript.

Head-quarters,
XXV th. DIVISIONAL CYCLIST COMPANY.
Army Form C. 2118

Place	Date March, 1916.	Hour	Summary of Events and Information	Remarks and references to Appendices
MERRIS. BUSMES.	1st.-9th. 10th.		In Rest Billet (2nd. Corps. Reserve) Paraded at 5-30 a.m. and marched via BLEU- NEUF BERQUIN - MERVILLE - ROBECQ - L'ECLEME to the Chateau de QUESNOY: 3/4 mile S. of BUSNES.	Capt. And
SACHIN	11th. 12th. 13th.		Paraded at 7-30 a.m. and marched via CANTRAINE - LILLERS - BURBURG- PERNES, to Sachin. In Billets. Long reconnaissance of XVII Corps area to area TINCQUES-HAUTE AVESNES- HABARCQ -AMBRINES.	
	14th-15th. 16th.		In Billets. Long reconnaissance to area HABARCQ - MAROOVIL -CARENCY - CAMBLAIN L'ABBE.	
BRYAS.	17th.		Paraded at 9 a.m. and marched via PERNES - VALHUON - BRYAS to L'ABBAYE de NEUVILLE farm about 1 mile E.S.E. of BRYAS.	
	18th-26th. 27th.		In Billets. Captn. R...Newton? Lieuts. W.G.Collins, F.B.RAYLY? 2/Lieut. A.M.C.Houghton,C.L.Blake R.Stephenson proceeded to Hd/Qrs. 7th. Brigade at CHELERS thence by motor charabancs to Mont ST ELOY. reconnoitred. Cirps Line from there to MAROEUIL. Returned by Charabancs.	
BRYAS	28th. 29th. 30th. 31st.		In Billets. Reconnaissance area CARENCY - CAMBLAIN L'ABBE - HABARCQ- MAROEUIL. In Billets. Paraded at 9-45 a.m. and marched via OSTREVILLE -MARQUAY, to part. in a scheme into E.Sqn. 1/1st. Lothians & Border Horse for Inspection by G.O.C. in C.	

Capt. Andrew(& 1 servant
A/ Staff Capt. 75th. Infy. Bde. 1-7.3.16.
1 Cpl. with7 men with 2nd. Field Survey Co. from 1-17th. 1 Cpl & 3 men, 17-20.
1 Cpl.& 2 men, 20-31st. 2 men Salvage Co. from 1st.-31st.; 4 men Sanitary Sec. 1st. -31st.
1 man Signal Coy. 1st-31st. 1 man Divsl. Grenade School, 1st.-30-31. 1 man Graves Registration.x.-31.
2 men ,198 Co. A.S.C. 1s t-31st. 1 man A.P.M.Orderly, 1st-31st. 1 Sergt. 6 men EscortG.O.C.
XVII Corps. 16th.-31st. Lieut. J.H.C.Lindesay, 1 Sgt. & 50 men Tre fic Road Control 22nd.,31st.
2 men D.A.D.O.S. 21st.- 31st. 2 Cpl. Railway Depot R.E.,1st.-31st.

(Sgnd.) R...Newton, Captain,
Commanding,XXV Divsnl.Cyclist Corps.

Certified True Copy
A.Manning Gen L.
Staff L. GHQ

25th. DIV. CYCLIST COY.

APRIL 1916.

Vol 7
2s Signal

Army Form C. 2118.

WAR DIARY
or
INTELLIGENCE SUMMARY. Reinft.
(Erase heading not required.)

APRIL 1916

Instructions regarding War Diaries and Intelligence Summaries are contained in F.S. Regs., Part II. and the Staff Manual respectively. Title pages will be prepared in manuscript.

Hour, Date, Place	Summary of Events and Information	Remarks and references to Appendices
BRYAS. 1st – 2nd April 1916	In Billets. (XVII Corps Reserve).	1 O. + 51. OR Road Traffic Control 1st – 2nd 1 O + 50. OR " " 3rd 9. OR " " 23rd 1. OR " " 24th
3rd April.	XVII Corps. Scheme for Corps Mounted Troops. Rendezvous at PENIN. (Strength of company, 5 of. 76 O Rs.).	
4th April 1916	Paraded at 1.15 p.m. and marched from L'ABBAYE de NEUVILLE farm via OSTREVILLE – MARQUAY – LIGNY ST FLOCHEL – to Billets at AVERDOINGT.	1 sgt + 6. OR Escort Duty G.O.C. – 14th 1 Man Signal Coy 25th Div – 13th 5 Men Sanitary Sec 25th Div – 30th
AVERDOINGT 5. April 16	In Billets.	25 – 30 2 " " – 30 2 Salvage Coy – 30
6. "	Capt RequitNewton + Lt Stephenson attended Corps Scheme at THELERS.	2 Bombing School – 30 1 " " – 30 2 D.A.D.O.S. – 30
7 – 12 Apr.	In Billets.	1 Orderly A.P.M. – 30 2 2nd Truck Convoy Coy 2nd Div – 30 1 A.S.C. 198 Coy A.S.C " – 30
12 Apr	Lieut W. E. COLLINS + 21 O.R. attended Steam Projector Demonstration – in Billets.	2 GRAVES Registration – 30 1 " On Command – 30 1 Officer + 6 O.R Observation Duties 25th Div from 21 – 30
18 Ap	Capt RequitNewton, Lt W.E.Collins, Mr Lindsay, F.S. Boyly Humphreys + R. Stephenson Attended a Smoke at BUNEVILLE. (D.O.R) Lamers Mounted Troops Div Mounted Troops	3 Guides R.T.O 27 – 30
	moved to Billets at BETHON- -ENCOURT — VILLERS-BRULIN	1 Officer + 65 OR Fatigue Duty BOMBING SCHOOL 25 Div 25-4-16 " " " 26 " 25/54 GO DR " " 27.4.16

Cabl...
COMMANDING,
XXVth DIVISIONAL CYCLIST COMPANY

[Stamp: 1 MAY 1916 HEADQUARTERS XXVth DIVISIONAL CYCLIST COMPANY]

www.ingramcontent.com/pod-product-compliance
Lightning Source LLC
Chambersburg PA
CBHW081252170426
43191CB00037B/2129